SECRETS OF Magic

INCREDIBLE ILLUSIONS

STEPHANIE TURNBULL

A⁺

Smart Apple Media

Published by Smart Apple Media
P.O. Box 3263
Mankato, MN 56002

Printed in the United States of America at Corporate Graphics,
in North Mankato, Minnesota.

Library of Congress Cataloging-in-Publication Data
Turnbull, Stephanie.
 Incredible illusions / by Stephanie Turnbull.
    p. cm. -- (Secrets of magic)
 Summary: "Reveals the secrets of famous illusions and teaches the skills needed
to perform illusions such as spoon-bending and levitation. Includes step-by-step
instructions, picture diagrams, and performance tips"--Provided by publisher.
 Includes index.
 ISBN 978-1-59920-497-0 (library binding)
 1. Magic tricks. I. Title.
 GV1547.T87 2012
 793.8--dc22

                                                      2010043375

Created by Appleseed Editions, Ltd.
Designed and illustrated by Guy Callaby
Edited by Mary-Jane Wilkins
Picture research by Su Alexander

Picture credits:
l = left, r = right, t = top, b = bottom
Contents page l Eline Spek/Shutterstock, r Ljupcosmokovski/Shutterstock; 4 Paris Pierce/Alamy;
5 Jon Bower London/Alamy; 6 RichardBaker/Alamy; 7 Bettmann/Corbis; 8 Inc/Shutterstock; 10 Stephen
Orsillo/Shutterstock; 12 Andrew Brusso/Corbis; 14 Karuka/Shutterstock; 16 Shutterstock; 18 Pixel 4
Images/Shutterstock; 19 Milos Luzanin/Shutterstock; 20 Aliaksei Sabelnikau/Shutterstock; 22l Mary Evans
Picture Library/Alamy, r Amy C Etra/Corbis; 23 INTERFOTO/Alamy; 24 Neil Guegan/Corbis;
25 The Protected Art Archive/Alamy; 26 Bernd Vogel/Corbis; 27 The Protected Art Archive/Alamy;
28t Kurhan/Shutterstock, b William Casey/Shutterstock; 29 Reuters/Corbis
Front cover: Pixel 4 Images/Shutterstock

DAD0049
3-2011

9 8 7 6 5 4 3 2 1

Contents

That's Impossible!

IF YOU WANT to become a magician, there are all kinds of incredible illusions you can do to amaze your friends. How about bending a spoon, stretching your thumb, or making a solid object rise from a table? Many illusions are actually very simple and easy to learn. You don't need many **props**, and you won't need to practice for years before you're ready to perform!

This poster for the magician Harry Kellar shows his **levitation** act. Read about levitation on pages 22–25.

FOOLING YOUR BRAIN

An illusion is an effect that tricks you into thinking that something impossible is happening. It works because you see something which your brain tries to process in a logical way, leaving you with a view or idea that can't be true. Here are two famous optical illusions.

Which of these yellow lines is longer?

In fact, the lines are the same length, but the top line looks longer. This is because your brain assumes that it is farther away, so it must be bigger. This is called the Ponzo Illusion.

What can you see here?

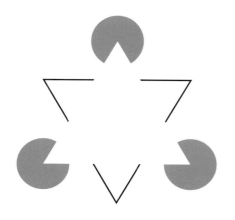

TRICK OF THE TRADE
If you want to specialize in illusions, try calling yourself an illusionist, not a magician. It sounds a lot more mysterious and exciting!

MAGIC IN ART

Optical illusions are often used in art to create certain effects. For example, cleverly-painted flat images can look like three-dimensional objects when you glance at them. This technique is called *trompe l'oeil*, which is French for "trick the eye." Some *trompe l'oeil* effects are small and subtle, such as a realistic-looking fly on a painting, while others are enormous—for example, a high church dome that is in fact a low, painted ceiling.

There seems to be a white triangle on top of a black-edged triangle, but in fact, no complete triangles are drawn. Your brain uses the bits of the picture that are drawn and fills in the gaps to make recognizable shapes. It is called the Kanizsa Triangle.

STAGE ILLUSIONS

Some magicians specialize in big illusions that involve assistants and complicated props. The illusions only work on a stage where the audience can't get too close because there are usually false doors, wires, or hidden assistants. Read about famous stage illusions on pages 22–27 and learn your own versions!

This large trompe l'oeil *sidewalk painting has been designed so that from the right angle, the girl looks as if she's really sitting on a high stool.*

MASTER MAGICIAN

JASPER MASKELYNE (1902–1973)

Jasper Maskelyne was an English magician whose father and grandfather were illusionists. During the Second World War, Maskelyne joined the army and formed a group called the Magic Gang, who created some of the biggest illusions ever. In North Africa, they created the illusion of a whole army to confuse the enemy. They made 2,000 fake tanks from plywood and built a realistic-looking railway line. In Egypt, they disguised the position of a city using lights and fake buildings in the sea. At night, the city seemed to be in a different place and confused bombers overhead.

Tricks of the Trade

THE KEY TO being a great illusionist is to remember three Ps: Practice, **Patter**, and Performance. Practice comes first. Even if a trick is simple, you need to practice until you know exactly what to do. Don't be tempted to try it out on people until it's perfect, or you risk giving away the secret. Once you've mastered a few tricks, you can think about your patter and performance. Here are some top tips.

PERFECT PATTER

Patter is what you say during a trick. Magicians who do big stage illusions often don't use much patter. All they need is dramatic music, sound effects, or lighting to keep their audience mesmerized. However, if you're performing small tricks in front of your family or friends, you'll need to talk to keep people entertained!

A good performance isn't just about tricks. The way you look, act, and talk is important too.

BE BOLD!

Imagine an actor who learned her lines perfectly but then stood awkwardly on stage and spoke in a flat voice. The audience wouldn't believe in the character the actor was playing, and they'd soon get bored, too! Being a magician is just the same. You need to act as though you're really bending a spoon or making something float, otherwise the illusion won't work. To do this well, you need lots of confidence.

Did I ever tell you how strong I am? Pass me your spoon and I'll demonstrate!

Patter helps to introduce illusions, such as spoon-bending (see pages 14–15), and also focuses your audience's attention.

FUNNY FORK

Here's a simple illusion to test your performance skills. It won't fool anyone for more than a few seconds, but it looks great!

1. Pick up a fork (or a knife or spoon) and say that you can make it defy gravity. Lay it across your left palm like this, and grab your wrist with your right hand.

2. Close your hand in a fist around the fork, and turn it around so the back faces the audience. As you turn it, straighten your right index finger to pin the fork against your palm.

*Talk while you do this. The patter helps **misdirect** people's attention from the position of your hands.*

audience view

back view

3. Hold up your hands and pretend to concentrate hard on the fork. Slowly and carefully, open your fingers one by one until just the thumb appears to be holding the fork. Then unbend your thumb too and spread your hand wide.

4. After a few seconds, close your hand quickly as if the fork is about to drop. Then sneak your index finger back down and turn your left hand around to show you're holding the fork as you did at the start.

MASTER MAGICIAN

HARRY BLACKSTONE, SR. (1888–1965)

Harry Blackstone, Sr. was one of the most famous illusionists ever. He performed elegant, flawless stage acts. One of his best-known effects was making a lighted bulb float around a darkened theater. Although his big illusions were performed to music, he was also skilled at small, **sleight-of-hand** tricks that allowed him to talk and joke with the audience. His patter was so good that he once persuaded everyone to stand up row by row and go outside to see the next illusion. Once they were on the street, they learned that the theater was on fire. Blackstone's calm, collected patter prevented a stampede and may have saved lives!

Harry Blackstone, Sr. (right) pretends to pull his assistant's head from a tube.

Clowning Around

THE GREAT THING about illusions is that they are entertaining to watch. Here are some funny and silly effects you could use at a party or to begin a stage act. You'll soon have your audience laughing, and they'll want to see more of your tricks.

*This girl is dressed as a **mime artist**. You can create funny illusions using mime.*

THE CRAZY CLIMBER

Try entering a room by climbing in sideways! The more effort you put into your acting, the funnier this looks.

1. Hide behind a doorway. Stand on one leg and bend over as far as you can, making the top half of your body horizontal. Lean into the wall to balance.

2. Throw one hand around the door frame and pretend to scramble for a handhold. Then do the same with the other hand. Haul yourself around the frame until your arms and head are in view. Make it look as if this is hard work!

3. For extra laughs, pretend to slip so that you disappear from sight.

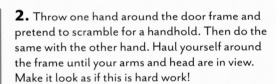

THE MYSTERY ARM

You try to enter the room again, but this time, a mysterious arm pulls you back!

1. Stand beside the doorway, making sure you keep one shoulder and arm hidden behind the wall. Chat with the audience, perhaps apologizing for your failed attempts to enter the room.

2. As you talk, grab your neck with the hand of your other arm. Look surprised as the mystery hand pulls you back behind the door frame!

Roll up your sleeve or wear a glove, so the arm doesn't look like yours.

3. For extra laughs, try coming back after a few moments having fought off your attacker only for the same thing to happen again!

THE MAGICAL HIDDEN ROOM

When you finally make it into the room, you could create more silly effects from behind a large sofa.

1. Say you need to fetch your props from a secret basement room. Go behind the sofa.

Make sure you hide your props behind the sofa before your audience arrives.

2. Pretend to walk down steps, crouching lower with each step. From the other side, it should look as though you're going downstairs.

3. Disappear from view, then come back up carrying your props. Or come up and down several times with different items!

MASTER MAGICIAN

PENN (born 1955) **AND TELLER** (born 1948)

Penn and Teller are magicians who are famous for their exciting, silly, and sometimes shocking tricks and pranks. They like to mix illusions and comedy to create stunning theater performances and TV shows. Penn trained as a clown and started out with a juggling act, while Teller is an expert at sleight-of-hand tricks. They make a funny double act because Penn is big, tall, and talkative, while Teller is smaller and hardly says a word. He uses mime instead.

Bendy Body Bits

WHY USE PROPS to perform illusions when you can appear to bend or stretch your own body? These effects are very simple, but you can make them look hilariously realistic. Keep a straight face and act the part, and soon you'll have everyone mesmerized!

Try to make your movements supple and graceful so people will be more likely to believe you have extra-bendy limbs!

MY THUMB CAME OFF!

1. Most body illusions are variations of the removable thumb trick. To do it, you need to bend both thumbs and hold them together in this position.

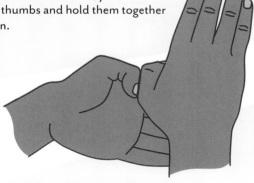

2. Cover the joint between your thumbs with the first two fingers of your right hand, like this.

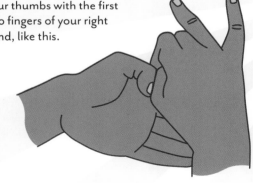

3. Here's what someone standing opposite you sees. They think there is just one thumb.

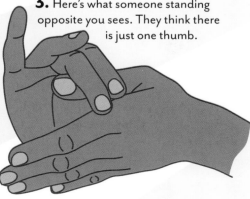

4. With a grunt of effort, pull your right hand away. It looks as if you've just removed the top of your thumb.

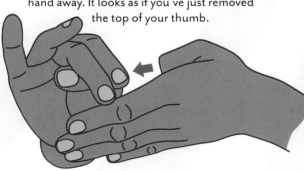

THE AMAZING STRETCHING THUMB
This illusion uses the same idea as the removable thumb.

TRICK OF THE TRADE
Grimace and gasp as you twist and bend your thumb as if it really hurts.

1. Stretch and flex your left hand a couple of times. Tell the audience that you have an amazingly stretchy thumb.

2. Grab your thumb with your right fist. As you do this, put your right thumb between your right index and middle fingers. It looks as though your left thumb is sticking up from your fist when in fact, it's the right thumb.

your view

audience view

3. Flex your left hand again and move your right thumb at the same time so it looks as if it's connected to the rest of the left hand.

4. Pretend to pull hard on your thumb. Slowly move your right hand up so it looks as if you're stretching your thumb. Every so often, flex your fingers and thumb so the thumb still looks connected. Keep going until just the tip of your left thumb is hidden under your fist.

5. Make the effect more appalling by pretending to twist your thumb around or bend it backward. When you've finished, slowly move your right hand back down and then whip it away to show that your thumb is back to normal. Phew!

EXTENDABLE ARM
Here's another stretchy body effect which is a simple optical illusion.
Make sure you're wearing a loose, long-sleeved shirt.

1. Before you begin, tug one sleeve as far down as you can. Hold your arm out to the side, but don't stretch it—you need to make it look short.

2. Say, "This new shirt is way too big. It's a good thing I've got a magical rubbery body. I can stretch it to fit!" Grab your fingers with your other hand and start pulling. Slowly let your arm move farther out of your sleeve.

3. As you pull, move your grabbing hand up your other hand and then to your wrist to create the illusion that your arm is growing longer. Stop when you've stretched your arm and pushed your shoulder forward as far as you can. Hold it and then let both arms drop. Adjust your shirt to show that it fits perfectly!

Yucky Stuff

Penn and Teller (see page 9) do lots of gory tricks, complete with fake blood.

IF YOU LIKED the body illusions, why not try a few really gruesome effects to make your friends squirm? You only need a few props. Just don't tell people what you're about to do. They'll be more grossed out if you surprise them.

PENCIL UP THE NOSE

This illusion is silly and fun. You need a long pencil, but make sure it's a plain color with no writing, stripes, or decoration.

1. Hold the pencil tip with your left hand and grab the end with your right hand.

Make sure you hold the pencil from underneath so the end is hidden in your right hand.

2. Hold the tip to a nostril. Then slowly slide your right hand up the pencil so it seems to move up your nose. The pencil should not move.

Pretend this is painful.

3. When you've finished, your right hand should be against your nose with hardly any pencil showing (it's hidden by your right hand and wrist).

4. Finish by slowly sliding your right hand back down the pencil as if you're drawing it out of your nose. Wipe it on your sleeve and hand it to your friend. Yuck!

TRICK OF THE TRADE

Try making the pencil come out of your ear. While it's hidden, quickly move both hands to one ear and pretend to draw out the pencil as you did from your nose.

Ow . . . I Bit My Finger Off!

Here's another brilliantly disgusting trick. This one relies on the awful noise of a crunching finger bone! You need to keep a straight face and do some great acting.

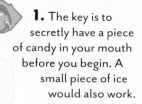

1. The key is to secretly have a piece of candy in your mouth before you begin. A small piece of ice would also work.

2. Start chewing a fingernail. Say, "I wish I could stop biting my nails. It's a horrible habit, but I can't help it!" As you talk, push your finger farther into your mouth and pretend you're chewing it.

3. As you chew, secretly move your finger between your teeth and your cheek so you're not really biting it. Push the candy or ice between your back teeth with your tongue. Then bite down hard to make a loud CRUNCH.

4. After a moment of shock, wince or cry out. You could then run out of the room holding your mouth or shrug and carry on munching as if you're enjoying the taste of your finger.

CRUNCH!

IMPORTANT!
Be careful not to break your teeth on hard candies. Use a cough drop or a mint with a soft center.

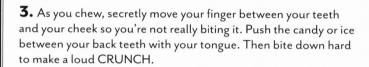

MASTER MAGICIAN

ALDO RICHIARDI, JR. (1923–1985)

Aldo Richiardi, Jr. was a Peruvian who shocked audiences with his yucky, scarily-realistic illusions. He often performed well-known tricks such as sawing a woman in half (see pages 26–27) but added fake blood to make the effect more gory. Unfortunately, after years of performing blood-soaked effects on stage and for television shows, poor Richiardi came to a grisly end himself. He injured his foot on stage, infection set in, and he died after having both legs amputated.

Spoon-Bending Skills

IF YOU WANT to be an illusionist, it's a good idea to learn a spoon-bending trick. In this illusion, you holds a solid piece of metal, such as a spoon or fork, and then uses the power of your mind and a few light touches to make the metal bend—or at least that's how it looks!

Magic Methods

The simplest way of making a piece of metal look wobbly and soft is to hold it loosely between your thumb and index finger and then waggle it up and down.

Another method is to weaken the handle of the spoon beforehand. Do this by bending it back and forth so that the metal is almost ready to break.

This takes a lot of practice. You might snap quite a few spoons before you get it right!

When you perform, hold the spoon at the weakened spot and rub it, pressing down slightly at the end of each stroke. The spoon should bend and snap. Cover the break with your fingers and let each end droop as if it's bending. Finally, let the spoon head fall off.

You'll be surprised at how effective this looks!

MASTER MAGICIAN

BANACHEK (born 1960)

Spoon-bending tricks are often done by magicians called **mentalists**. Banachek is a famous mentalist who seems to make metal wilt and bend like spaghetti as soon as he touches it. His tricks are so effective that many people are convinced he really does have strange powers. In fact, he uses sleight-of-hand moves and brilliant misdirection techniques, but of course he always keeps his methods secret.

TRICK OF THE TRADE
Cheap, thin teaspoons work best. Buy a set of the cheapest spoons you can find rather than ruining ones at home!

HANDS-ON SPOON-BENDING

Pretend to bend a spoon without doing a thing. Perform this at a table with your audience sitting opposite you.

1. Before you start, secretly hold a small silver coin, such as a dime, in your right hand.

rim of coin

2. Pick up a teaspoon with the other hand and say, "Look how thin the spoons are here!" Now grab it with both hands. As you do this, push up the coin slightly so that it looks like the top of the handle.

Make sure your hands overlap, or the spoon will look too long.

3. Pretend to press forward and bend the spoon. Let the handle of the spoon slowly slide down through your hands. As your hands move forward and the spoon moves back, you seem to bend it.

side view

4. When you've "bent" the spoon as far as you can, say, "Wait a minute, I don't want to get into trouble . . . it's a good thing I can unbend metal too!" Toss the spoon on the table. While everybody's looking at it, sneak the coin on to your lap.

HANDS-OFF SPOON-BENDING

With this trick, you end up with a bent spoon that people can marvel at. It takes a lot of practice.

1. Find two identical teaspoons with short handles. Bend one until the head breaks off, and bend the other into a right angle. Put the bent spoon and the broken handle in your pocket.

2. Put the spoons in position under the table. First, hold the bent spoon so the head hangs down and the handle is hidden in your hand.

broken-off handle

bent spoon

3. Take the broken handle and grip it upright with your thumb and index finger so it appears to be connected to the spoon head.

4. Hold up the spoon and say you can bend it with the power of your mind without touching it. Concentrate and stroke the air over the spoon. Slowly loosen your grip on the handle and let it fall backward.

This part of your hand hides the broken handle.

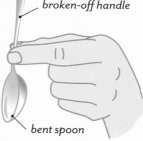

5. Let the handle fall until it rests on your hand. Your hand hides the broken handle. Now pull out the bent spoon.

6. Hold up the bent spoon or pass it around. As you do, move your right hand under the table and drop the handle in your lap.

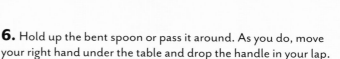

Pranks with Props

YOU CAN PERFORM brilliant illusions with all kinds of everyday items. Here is a selection of quick tricks that use simple, easily available props. They work well as one-off jokes, or you could include them in a bigger stage act.

Here are some of the things you will need to perform these effects.

THE FAKE PAPER TEAR

Make sure you try this sneaky torn paper illusion on someone who can take a joke!

1. Take a folded sheet of newspaper and tear a tiny triangle from the margin.

2. Crinkle up half of the triangle so that it stands out.

3. Moisten the flat half and stick it on your mom's new wallpaper or your friend's best painting. It looks just like a tear!

THE GLASS GUESSING GAME

There's no secret behind this illusion. It's a good example of how your eyes can fool you!

1. Put a glass in front of you. Ask your friends to guess which they think is the greater distance: around the rim of the glass or from the top of the glass to the table.

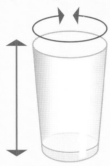

The vertical measurement looks much longer. Some people might think it's a trick and that the two are the same.

2. Put a slim book or a pack of cards under the glass and ask them which distance is greater now: around the rim, or from the top of the glass to the table. Then add a few more books and ask again.

By this time, everyone will be sure that the vertical measurement is longer.

3. Reveal the truth by measuring the rim with a piece of string and then holding the string vertically against the glass. To everyone's amazement, the distance around the rim is greater than its height!

TRICK OF THE TRADE
Beforehand, work out how many books you can put under the glass while making sure the measurement around the rim is greater.

THE BOUNCING APPLE

Use this illusion at a table. You need to be on the opposite side of your audience for it to work. It relies on great timing, so practice in front of a mirror until you've perfected it.

1. Sit sideways at the table with an apple and pretend to throw the apple toward the ground as if it's a ball. Don't let go of it!

2. As your arm moves below the table, stamp your foot to sound like the apple hitting the floor. Immediately, toss the apple into the air, keeping your hand hidden and your arm as straight as possible.

Toss the apple in the air . . .

3. If you time it right, the apple should appear to bounce up off the floor.

. . . just after stamping your foot.

audience view

Tactile Tricks

NOT ALL ILLUSIONS are visual. Many weird and wonderful illusions work by fooling your sense of touch. Have you ever worn a hat for a long time and then taken it off but felt that there was still something on your head? That is a **tactile** illusion.

You might be surprised at how often your brain interprets sensations wrongly when you can't see what's going on.

FINGERS CROSSED

One famous tactile effect is called the **Aristotle Illusion**. Ask a friend to cross their index and second fingers and close their eyes. Touch a pencil to the tips of their crossed fingers. Ask them how many pencils they feel. Most people think there are two. This is because the brain is fooled by the unfamiliar position of the fingers.

ONE TOUCH OR TWO?

Here's another tactile illusion that works because your sense of touch is better in some parts of the body than others. Ask a friend to pull up a sleeve, hold out an arm, and close their eyes. Take two pencils and grip them so the points are about 1/2 inch (1 cm) apart. Touch your friend's arm near the elbow with both points at once and ask them how many are touching them. Most people only feel one.

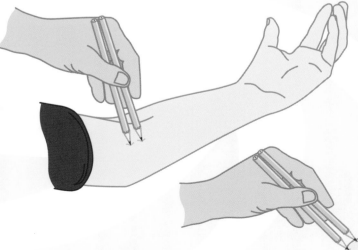

Now touch the tip of their index finger with the two pencils. The person should feel two points now as this part of the body is more sensitive.

VIRTUAL REALITY HAND

This illusion was discovered by scientists studying how the brain works. The original experiment used a fake hand, but you can use a rubber glove instead. Blow it full of air and tie the wrist, or stuff it with cotton balls.

1. Sit a friend at a table with their hands out in front of them. Shield their left hand from their view with a screen—for example, a big book or a cereal box on its side, and place the rubber hand in sight on the other side of the screen. Drape a cloth over the end of the fake hand and the person's left arm.

cloth

cereal box

fake hand

The key is to make the rubber hand seem to be your friend's left hand.

Ask your friend to keep looking at the rubber hand.

2. Stand behind your friend's left shoulder with a small paintbrush in each hand. Stroke the real left hand and the rubber hand with the brushes, making exactly the same movements on each. Go slowly up and down each finger and tap the brushes in identical places on each hand.

TRICK OF THE TRADE

Although this doesn't work on everyone, it's more likely to work if your friend concentrates on the rubber hand. Help them by making sure you're in a quiet place. Be serious, but also confident and relaxed as if you know the illusion will work.

3. After a few minutes, your friend should start to feel as if the rubber hand is their own hand. You can test this by banging the rubber hand or touching a hot cup to the rubber fingertips. The person may flinch as if the sensation is real.

Ask your friend to try the trick on you afterward so you can experience it too.

I'm Strong . . . You're Weak

WOULD YOU LIKE to have superhuman strength while everyone around you becomes impossibly weak? Some tricks use laws of physics to create amazing illusions of extreme strength or weakness. Here are a few to try. They are most effective when demonstrated on people bigger than you.

TRICK OF THE TRADE

Before you start, you could pretend to use magic words or **hypnotism** to turn everybody into weaklings. You could perform dressed as a superhero. It all adds to the entertainment!

Do some warm-up exercises first to make it look as if you need extreme strength for these tricks.

ARMS OF STEEL

1. Boast that your arms are so strong that no one can pull them apart. Put your fists together like this.

2. Ask someone to grab you above the elbows and try to pull your fists apart. They won't be able to!

*This works because the muscle group you use to push your fists together has more **leverage** than the muscles your friend has to use.*

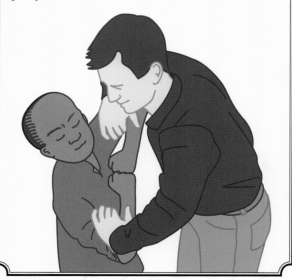

SUPERHUMAN THUMB

Here's another leverage trick. Start by explaining that you have an extraordinarily strong thumb.

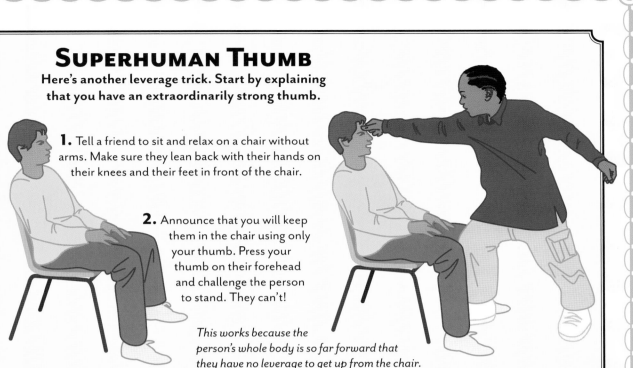

1. Tell a friend to sit and relax on a chair without arms. Make sure they lean back with their hands on their knees and their feet in front of the chair.

2. Announce that you will keep them in the chair using only your thumb. Press your thumb on their forehead and challenge the person to stand. They can't!

This works because the person's whole body is so far forward that they have no leverage to get up from the chair.

THE IMPOSSIBLE FOOT-LIFT

Introduce this trick by saying, "Can you lift your right leg off the ground and hold it in the air? OK, let's see . . ."

1. Ask a friend to stand with the side of their left foot and their left cheek pressed against a wall.

2. Tell them all they have to do is lift their right foot up off the ground for 5 seconds. It sounds simple . . . but they won't be able to do it!

The position of the body against the wall means they can't lift the outer leg.

LULU HURST (1869–1950)

Lulu Hurst came from Georgia. When she was 14, she began demonstrating amazing strength. For example, she could prevent a strong man from holding a stick steady or make herself so heavy that he couldn't lift her. These were all leverage and balance tricks, combined with spooky acting which convinced her audiences that she had mysterious gifts. One famous routine was to tip a heavy man off a chair even though he was trying to stay on. Can you guess how she did it? Find the answer on page 32.

Nicknamed the "Georgia Wonder," Lulu Hurst performed across America, but her fame didn't last. Soon people began to reveal her secrets, and other women began copying her act. She was only 16 when she retired from the stage forever.

Levitation Tricks

IF YOU WATCH an illusionist performing on stage or television, it won't be long before you see a levitation trick. Levitation is the effect of suspending someone or something in the air without any visible support so they appear to defy gravity. Done well, it looks spectacular.

David Copperfield (see page 29) performs a levitation trick. From where the audience is sitting, he seems to be floating in midair without support.

SECRETS OF THE EXPERTS

When magicians levitate on stage, you can be sure they are using thin wires or other supports that are either hidden from view or too thin to be seen from where the audience is sitting. It's even easier on TV as magicians can use camera trickery to hide certain things from view or edit footage to make it look as if something impossible just happened.

*This is an old, famous levitation effect performed by Indian **yogis**. A thin seat sticks out from the pole and is hidden under the man's long robes.*

No-Strings Levitation

Without expensive props, you can't rise to the ceiling or float around, but you can appear to rise a few centimeters off the ground. This surprisingly effective illusion works well in a dimly-lit room or outside at dusk.

audience view

1. Make sure your audience is well away from you. Stand in an open space and show that there are no wires or hidden supports around you.

2. Stand with your feet together and at an angle so that no one can see your left foot. Keep your legs straight and slowly rise up on your left toes. At the same time, lift your whole right foot.

Keep your heels together and make sure the angle of your feet hides your left toes so it looks as though both feet rise off the ground.

3. Hold it for a couple of seconds. Then lower your feet to the ground again.

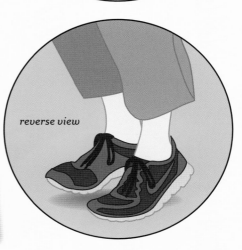

reverse view

TRICK OF THE TRADE
If people are impressed, they'll ask you to do it again. DON'T! If you repeat a trick people will look much harder to work out how you did it.

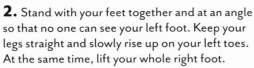
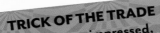

MASTER MAGICIAN

SERVAIS LE ROY (1865–1953)

Servais Le Roy was a Belgian magician who performed large-scale illusions. One was a levitation effect known as Asrah the Floating Princess, which he performed with his wife, Talma. Talma lay on a couch and Le Roy covered her with a cloth. She levitated and floated in the air for a few moments before sinking back on to the couch. Le Roy whipped off the cloth and Talma had disappeared.

The equipment for the trick was complicated and included a wire frame, which was kept locked away so no one would discover how it worked.

More Midair Magic

IT'S NOT JUST people who can levitate. Magicians often make solid objects rise gracefully into the air and then float or dance around the stage. These tricks are performed using hidden wires, supports, magnets, or extra-thin thread. Here are a few famous floating illusions plus one you can do yourself.

This glowing ball seems to hover in the air. Magicians often use their body position or spooky lighting effects to hide wires or supports.

THE ZOMBIE BALL

One of the best-known floating illusions is the zombie ball. A silvery metal ball rests on a stand in the middle of the stage. When the magician covers the ball with a silk cloth, it begins to float upward. It then darts and dances in the air as the magician holds the corners of the cloth. The secret is a hidden support under the cloth. Try it with a bread roll and learn how it's done!

THE ZOMBIE BREAD ROLL

This illusion is ideal for performing in a restaurant. All you need is a bread roll and a large cloth napkin plus a fork as your hidden support.

1. Position a fork on the table near your right hand. If there are lots of things on the table, nobody will notice it. Begin the trick by putting a bread roll on the table. Take a folded napkin, shake it out dramatically, and drape it over the roll. Make sure it covers the fork.

2. With your right hand, grab one edge of the napkin and the end of the fork handle. With your left hand, pretend to check that the roll is in place under the napkin. In fact, your hand holds the roll as you spear it with the fork.

3. Hold the left corner of the napkin with your left hand. Now pretend to concentrate on the roll. Very slowly and steadily, move the fork upward so that the roll appears to be rising under the cloth.

4. Now make the roll move in different directions, sometimes suddenly, as if it has a mind of its own.

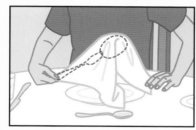

You'll need to practice this to do it quickly and easily.

Always move both hands together so no one will notice you're doing something with your right hand.

The better your acting skills, the better this will look!

5. Let the roll slowly fall back to the table. Clamp your left hand on top as if to stop it from rising again. This gives you a chance to pull out the fork with your right hand and whip the napkin (with the fork underneath) on to your lap.

TRICK OF THE TRADE
Hide the roll afterward so people don't notice the fork holes, or disguise them by breaking open the roll to prove there are no hidden wires or threads inside.

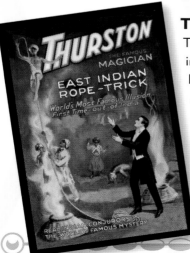

THE INDIAN ROPE TRICK

The Indian rope trick is a famous illusion in which a rope snakes out of a basket and hangs in the sky while someone climbs it. Although it is supposed to be an ancient trick, many people believe that it was never really performed in the past and that it is only recently that magicians have found ways to enact it. The methods used are a well-kept secret but probably involve trick ropes, wires, or clever camera work.

Sawing Illusions

PERHAPS THE MOST famous stage illusion of all involves a magician sawing his or her assistant in half. The assistant lies inside a large wooden box with his or her head and feet sticking out. After the box is cut, the two halves are moved apart and then put back together, after which the assistant climbs out, unharmed.

A magician performs the sawing illusion. How do you think this one might be done?

THE FIRST SAWING TRICK

The sawing illusion was first performed in 1921 by English magician P. T. Selbit. He tied up a woman with rope and locked her in a crate. Volunteers held the ends of the rope while the magician sawed through the crate with a large hand saw. The audience had never seen such an exciting trick! Soon other magicians were performing their versions, and today, there are all kinds of sawing illusions.

SAWING SECRETS

The key to the trick is the box. It could be wider than the audience can see, so the assistant has room to curl up in the top half, leaving their boots sticking out of the end of the box. Sometimes the box has fake feet that extend through the foot holes when the assistant climbs in and activates them.

Another method is to have a hollow table under the box that the assistant stretches out in. Some versions have a second assistant hiding in the lower half of the box, ready to stick their feet through the holes when the first assistant lies down.

Many modern illusionists have developed new twists on the old methods that are much harder to figure out.

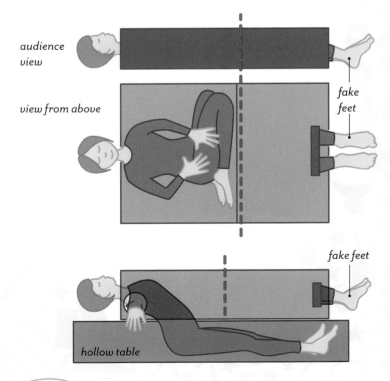

audience view

view from above

fake feet

fake feet

hollow table

SEVERED BY SCISSORS

Here's a great way of performing your own sawing illusion.

TRICK OF THE TRADE
You could cut out a photo of someone and stick it on the card or use a photo of a friend's face.

1. Beforehand, cut two slits in the front of an envelope. Cut a piece of card narrower than the envelope but long enough to stick out at both ends.

2. Draw a person (your assistant) on the card, or ask a volunteer to do so. Announce that you will saw the person in half.

3. Take the envelope and seal it. Then cut off both ends with scissors. Make sure no one sees the slits on the other side.

4. Put your assistant in the envelope. Push the card through each slit so the middle section is behind the envelope. *Practice this. The card must seem to go smoothly through the envelope.*

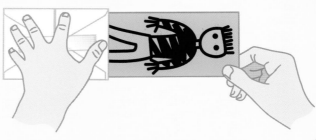

view from underneath　　　　　*audience view*

5. Take your saw (scissors) and make a big deal of cutting the envelope in half. Cut just the envelope—not the card behind.

Keep both sides of the envelope together, or you may reveal the uncut card behind.

6. Hold the two halves of the envelope still and dramatically pull out the card. Your assistant is still whole!

MASTER MAGICIAN

HORACE GOLDIN (1873–1939)

Horace Goldin was born in Lithuania but moved to the United States when he was 16. He became known as the "Whirlwind Illusionist," rapidly performing trick after trick without speaking. Disaster struck in 1918 when a boat carrying his money and stage props sank. It seemed that his career was over, but then he saw P. T. Selbit's sawing illusion. Goldin created his own version in which the assistant's head and feet stuck out of the box. This made the illusion much more impressive. Goldin soon became rich and far more famous than Selbit.

Show Time!

ONCE YOU'VE PERFECTED a few illusions, you can perform them as one-off tricks to entertain your friends or family during meals or at parties. Alternatively, you may want to try staging a magic show to impress a larger audience. Here are some hints and tips to help make your show a success.

Have fun with your costume! Look in charity shops for quirky clothes, or try making your own outfit.

PERFORM IN STYLE

The way you look is an important part of the show. You could grab attention by creating an air of mystery—wear a cloak or mask, and dim the lights. Or dress as a clown, use **slapstick** comedy, and act as if you have no control over the impossible things that happen! Decide on a style you're comfortable with and make sure that every part of your act—costume, patter, props, and so on—suits the theme.

DISASTER!

If something goes wrong—say, you drop a hidden, pre-bent spoon out of your sleeve—move on to the next trick quickly. Make a joke if that suits your act, but don't apologize or get flustered. If you stay cool and act confidently, people may even wonder if the mistake was part of the act!

Many illusions only work from a certain angle, so make sure you work out what your audience will be able to see.

Some performers, such as this carnival magician, dress in dazzling robes and masks.

WHAT'S ON THE END OF THE ROPE?

This illusion is designed to be performed on a stage.
You'll need a rope and two assistants.

1. Your assistants need to stand out of sight on either side of the stage. One assistant holds the rope. Come on stage pulling the rope as if there is something heavy on the end.

The audience can't see what's happening behind the curtains.

2. Cross the stage. When you're out of sight, hand the rope to the second assistant and run behind the stage to the other side. The second assistant keeps pulling, so it looks as if you're still walking.

3. Now take the end of the rope from the first assistant. Let the second assistant pull you on to the stage, so it looks as though the weight you were pulling was you!

MASTER MAGICIAN

DAVID COPPERFIELD (born 1956)

David Copperfield began performing magic tricks when he was 12. He went on to become a world famous illusionist, starring in TV programs and touring the world with spectacular stage shows. His illusions are huge, dramatic, and completely over the top—for example, levitating across the Grand Canyon, flying through the air, and making the Statue of Liberty disappear. According to him, each new illusion takes about two and a half years to create, and the flying trick took seven years.

Glossary

Aristotle Illusion
a tactile illusion that is said to have been discovered by the ancient Greek philosopher Aristotle

hypnotism
the act of putting someone into a kind of trance in which they can often be persuaded to alter their behavior or thoughts

leverage
forcing something to move by working like a mechanical lever; The more leverage you can use, the easier it is to move or lift something.

levitation
the process of suspending something or someone without any support so they defy gravity; Objects can genuinely levitate using magnets and other scientific methods, but in magic acts, the levitation is usually a trick.

mentalist
someone who performs a kind of magic called mentalism, in which things seem to happen because of a person's amazing mental powers; Mentalism tricks include bending spoons, reading minds, and communicating using thoughts.

mime artist
someone who performs using mime, which means acting out stories using body movements instead of speech

misdirect
to draw an audience's attention away from something you don't want them to see or think too much about

patter
prepared, practiced speech that magicians use when performing magic tricks; Although you need to work out your patter beforehand, make sure you speak naturally and don't read it out like a script.

prop
short for "property;" any object that is used to help perform a trick

slapstick
silly, funny, and over the top; Clowns often perform slapstick comedy, for example chasing around or pretending to slip on banana skins.

sleight-of-hand
the technique of secretly moving, altering, or swapping objects to create a magical effect; Sleights (pronounced "slights") take a lot of practice to perform well and rely on good misdirection skills.

tactile
to do with the sense of touch

yogi
someone who is a master of yoga, which includes meditation and philosophy

Web Sites

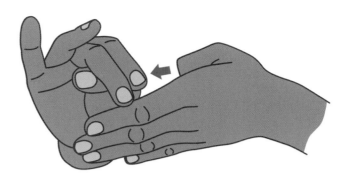

www.magictricks.com/library
Read biographies of famous magicians and discover fascinating facts about their lives and the tricks they invented.

www.geniimagazine.com/wiki/index.php/Category:Illusions
Find links to information about all kinds of classic stage illusions, including levitation, the Indian rope trick, sawing someone in half, and many more.

http://kids.niehs.nih.gov/illusion/illusions.htm
Be amazed by lots of fantastic optical illusions.

www.freemagictricks4u.com/spoon-bending.html
Watch helpful video tutorials that show you how to perform the great spoon-bending tricks on page 15.

www.magicsam.com/index.asp
Find out about The Society of American Magicians, the oldest magical society in the world, which was once headed by Harry Houdini. Read about recent magic news and find S. A. M. assemblies in your area!

www.magician.org/
Learn about the history of the International Brotherhood of Magicians, the world's largest organization for those interested in or practicing magic. Find magic shows, lectures, and conventions near you!

Index

SECRETS OF MAGIC . . . REVEALED!

Page 21: How did Lulu Hurst manage to tip the heavy man off his chair?

Answer: The key to this trick was the position the man sat in. Because he was trying to resist being tipped over, he automatically planted his feet firmly on the floor, thus moving most of his weight to his feet rather than on the chair. This meant that it wasn't too hard for Lulu Hurst to tip the chair slightly, which she did by crouching behind it, bracing her arms against her knees, and pushing. As the man tried to change position to counter the tip, she suddenly relaxed her arms, making him lose his balance, and then she quickly tipped the chair again in another direction. Before long, she made him fall off the chair altogether!